Riverbo

Original story by Leanne Miles
Illustrated by Sue O'Loughlin and John Dunne

Riverboat Bill doesn't live in a house.
He lives on a boat with his cat, Morris.
The name of the boat is Sarah Lou.

Today Riverboat Bill and Morris are
sailing on a river in India. There are
tigers and monkeys in India.

3

Riverboat Bill has got a big nose and a brown moustache. He wears glasses and a white cap. He likes sailing his boat on the river and he likes singing.

♪♪♪ *Mississippi, Amazon,*
River Thames too.
I sail on them all ♪♪♪
In my good boat, Sarah Lou.

Riverboat Bill and Morris sail to lots
of countries.
One day, they sail to Australia. There are
kangaroos in Australia.

Suddenly, Riverboat Bill sees something in
the water. He pokes it with his pole.

But it isn't a tree at all. It's a …

… crocodile!

There are crocodiles in Australia too!

It's an enormous crocodile with a long tail and very big teeth.

It's lunchtime. I'm hungry!

Next, Riverboat Bill and Morris sail
to Africa.
Riverboat Bill sees something in the water.
He pokes it with his pole.

What's this?
Is it a rock?

Suddenly, a very big mouth comes out
of the water.

11

Finally, Riverboat Bill and Morris sail to the Caribbean. They see something in the water.

What's this? Is it a pole? I need a new pole.

But it isn't a pole at all. It's a ...

… periscope!

It's Submarine Stan and he's very angry.

15

So Riverboat Bill and Morris the cat sail back to the river again.

Activities

1 Read and match.

a
What's this?
Is it a tree?

b
That's not a rock!
It's a hippo and
it's got your pole!

c
What's this?
Is it a pole?
I need a new
pole.

d
It's lunchtime.
I'm hungry!

e
I'm fishing.

f
Oops!
Sorry Stan!

1 _e_

2 ____

3 ____

4 ____

5 ____

6 ____

2 Look and colour.

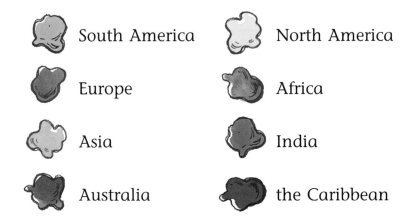

South America   North America

Europe   Africa

Asia   India

Australia   the Caribbean

3 Find and write.

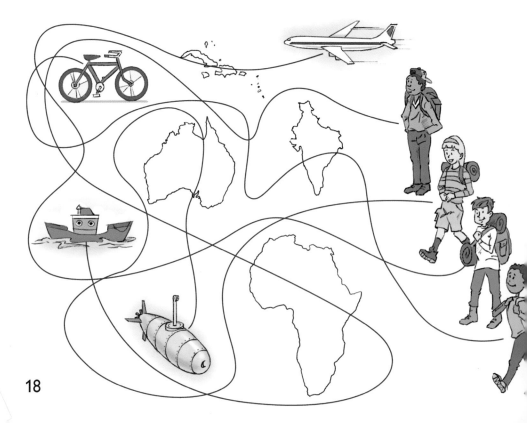

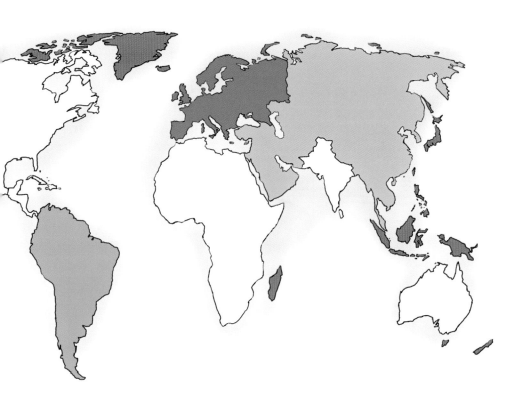

1 He's going to ___Africa___ by ___boat___.

2 She's going to _____ by _____.

3 _____.

4 _____.

4 Read and match.

1 Riverboat Betty has got short, blonde hair and green eyes. She wears small glasses and a white cap. ☐

2 Riverboat Brian has got straight, black hair and brown eyes. He hasn't got a moustache. He's got a red and white T-shirt. ☐

a

c

b

3 Riverboat Brenda has got long, blonde hair and blue eyes. She wears big glasses and a white cap. ☐

d

4 Riverboat Bruce has got curly, black hair and brown eyes. He's got a black moustache. ☐

5 Write.

Riverboat Bill has got _____

_____

_____

_____

_____.

6 Spot the differences. Write.

A  B

1 In picture A _there is a submarine in the river_ .
  In picture B _there is a boat on the river_ .

2 In picture A there are three _____birds_____ .
  In picture B there is one _____ .

3 In picture A there are _____ butterflies.
  In picture B there are _____ butterflies.

4 In picture A there is a _____ in the river.
  In picture B there is a _____ in the river.

5 In picture A _____ .
  In picture B _____ .

6 In picture A _____ .
  In picture B _____ .

Picture Dictionary

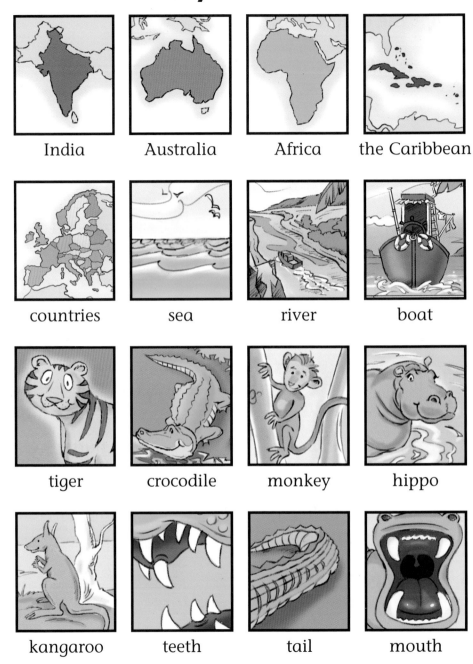

India   Australia   Africa   the Caribbean

countries   sea   river   boat

tiger   crocodile   monkey   hippo

kangaroo   teeth   tail   mouth

submarine

periscope

pole

rock

to sail

to sing

to poke

to fish

hungry

angry

water

long

nose

moustache

cap

glasses

tree

Macmillan Education
Between Towns Road, Oxford OX4 3PP
A division of Macmillan Publishers Limited
Companies and representatives throughout the world

ISBN-13: 978-1-4050-2506-5
ISBN-13: 978-1-4050-5728-8 (International Edition)

First published 2002 Macmillan Education Australia Pty Ltd
This edition © Macmillan Publishers Limited 2004

Illustrated by Sue O'Loughlin and John Dunne.

Printed and bound in China

2012 2011 2010
10   Spain
10   International